W9-CLI-836

DISASTER ZONE
BLIZZARDS

by Cari Meister

pogo

Ideas for Parents and Teachers

Pogo Books let children practice reading informational text while introducing them to nonfiction features such as headings, labels, sidebars, maps, and diagrams, as well as a table of contents, glossary, and index.

Carefully leveled text with a strong photo match offers early fluent readers the support they need to succeed.

Before Reading

- "Walk" through the book and point out the various nonfiction features. Ask the student what purpose each feature serves.
- Look at the glossary together. Read and discuss the words.

Read the Book

- Have the child read the book independently.
- Invite him or her to list questions that arise from reading.

After Reading

- Discuss the child's questions. Talk about how he or she might find answers to those questions.
- Prompt the child to think more. Ask: Have you ever been in a blizzard? How long did it last? What did you do?

Pogo Books are published by Jump!
5357 Penn Avenue South
Minneapolis, MN 55419
www.jumplibrary.com

Library of Congress Cataloging-in-Publication Data

Meister, Cari.
  Blizzards / by Cari Meister.
      pages cm – (Disaster zone)
  Includes index.
  Audience: 7-10.
  ISBN 978-1-62031-223-0 (hardcover: alk. paper) –
  ISBN 978-1-62031-263-6 (paperback) –
  ISBN 978-1-62496-310-0 (ebook)
  1. Blizzards–Juvenile literature. I. Title.
  QC926.37.M45 2016
  551.55'5–dc23
                                                2014044359

Series Editor: Jenny Fretland VanVoorst
Series Designer: Anna Peterson
Photo Researcher: Anna Peterson

Photo Credits: Connecticut State Library/Flickr, 17; Dreamstime, 6-7, 11, 14-15; Glow Images, 20-21; iStock, 18-19; Shutterstock, cover, 1, 3, 4, 8-9, 10, 12-13, 16; Thinkstock, 5, 23.

Printed in the United States of America at Corporate Graphics in North Mankato, Minnesota.

TABLE OF CONTENTS

CHAPTER 1

IT'S A BLIZZARD!

Imagine you are sitting in a classroom in Colorado. You look out the window.

There is snow everywhere. The wind is blowing. You cannot see anything but white. It's a blizzard!

You go home early.

Blizzards make it hard
to travel. The blowing
snow makes it hard to
see the road. Cars slide.
Some end up in the **ditch**.

Luckily, you make
it home safely.

When large amounts of snow fall, it is called a snowstorm. Blizzards often start out as snowstorms.

DID YOU KNOW?

Sometimes, blizzards happen a day or two after the snow has fallen. The wind is so strong that it looks like it is snowing.

CHAPTER 2

HOW DO BLIZZARDS FORM?

A snowstorm needs cold air, lots of **moisture**, and **lift**.

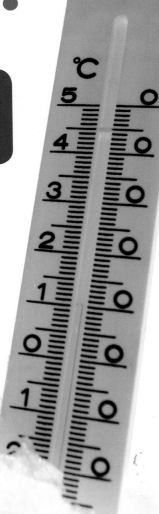

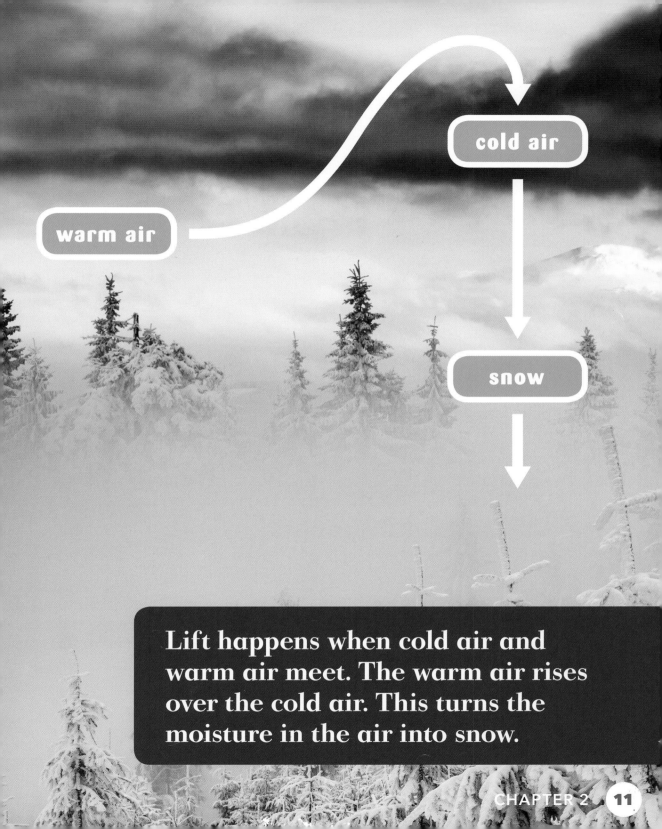

warm air

cold air

snow

Lift happens when cold air and warm air meet. The warm air rises over the cold air. This turns the moisture in the air into snow.

But a blizzard is different from a snowstorm. A snowstorm becomes a blizzard when it has four things.

1) There must be heavy or blowing snow.

2) Wind speeds must be greater than 35 miles per hour (56 kilometers per hour).

3) **Visibility** must be less than a quarter of a mile (.4 km).

4) The **duration** must be longer than three hours.

In the United States, blizzards are common on mountaintops and on the Northern **Great Plains**.

Blizzards also happen along the Northeast Coast and near the **Great Lakes**.

Lake Michigan

WHERE DO THEY HAPPEN?

Blizzards are common in the Great Plains. The cold, dry weather creates light, fluffy snow. The flat land allows for high wind speeds. Together they create perfect blizzard conditions.

UNITED STATES

■ = Blizzard Zones

CHAPTER 3

DEADLY BLIZZARDS

The deadliest blizzard in history happened in 1972 in **Iran**. More than 25 feet (7.6 meters) of snow fell, and 4,000 people died.

During the Great Blizzard of 1888, more than 400 Americans along the East Coast lost their lives.

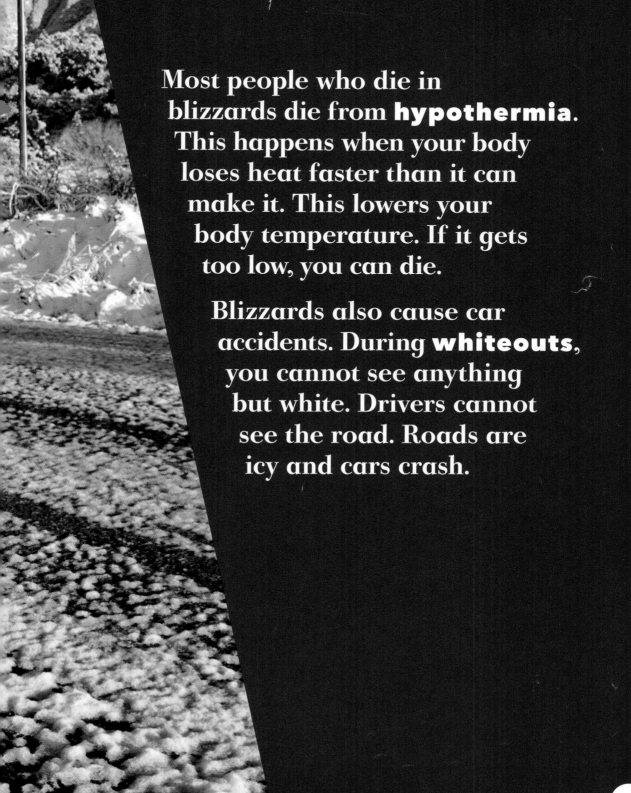

Most people who die in blizzards die from **hypothermia**. This happens when your body loses heat faster than it can make it. This lowers your body temperature. If it gets too low, you can die.

Blizzards also cause car accidents. During **whiteouts**, you cannot see anything but white. Drivers cannot see the road. Roads are icy and cars crash.

To stay safe in a blizzard, stay inside. If you have to go out, dress warmly. Keep water, blankets, food, and warm clothes in your car.

If you're prepared, a blizzard doesn't need to be dangerous. So bundle up, and let it snow!

DID YOU KNOW?

An emergency kit is helpful in any disaster. It should include:

- Water
- Canned or dried food (and a can opener)
- First aid kit
- Cell phone and charger
- Radio
- Blankets

ACTIVITIES & TOOLS

TRY THIS!

SNOWSTORM IN A CAN

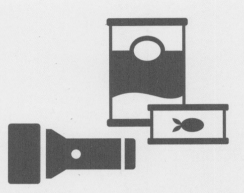

What You Need:
- two cans—one large, one small
- ice
- salt
- dry ice
- towel
- flashlight

1. Mix ice with salt and put it in the large can.

2. Put the small can on the ice so that its top is level with the top of the large can.

3. Pack salt and ice in the space between the two cans.

4. The large can will get very cold. Put a towel around it.

5. The air in the small can will get cold. When this happens, breathe into the small can.

6. This will form a small cloud. Now, shave off small pieces of dry ice and drop them on the cloud.

7. Shine the flashlight into the cloud. You will see small crystals of ice.

8. Breathe into the cloud to give it moisture. Wait a minute, and then breathe into it again.

9. Keep breathing into the cloud until the crystals fall as snow!

GLOSSARY

ditch: The low spot next to a road.

duration: The amount of time something takes.

Great Lakes: Five large lakes near the border of Canada and the United States; they are Lake Huron, Lake Erie, Lake Superior, Lake Michigan, and Lake Ontario.

Great Plains: A large area of flat grassland in the United States that lies between the Mississippi River and the Rocky Mountains.

hypothermia: A dangerous condition when a person's body temperature goes too low.

Iran: A mountainous country in the Middle East.

lift: When warm air rises over cold air.

moisture: Water in the air.

whiteout: When the wind blows a large amount of snow and you cannot see.

visibility: How far you can see in bad weather conditions.

INDEX

TO LEARN MORE

Learning more is as easy as 1, 2, 3.

1) Go to www.factsurfer.com

2) Enter "blizzards" into the search box.

3) Click the "Surf" to see a list of websites.

With factsurfer, finding more information is just a click away.